THE TORTOISE HAD A MIGHTY ROAR

Poems by **Peter Dixon**

Illustrated by **David Thomas**

First published 2005 by Macmillan Children's Books
a division of Macmillan Publishers Limited
20 New Wharf Road, London N1 9RR
Basingstoke and Oxford
www.panmacmillan.com

Associated companies throughout the world

ISBN 0 330 41799 1

Text copyright © Peter Dixon 2005

The right of Peter Dixon and Jamas to be identified as the
author and illustrator of this work has been asserted by them in accordance with
the Copyright, Designs and Patents Act 1988.

1 3 5 7 9 8 6 4 2

A CIP catalogue record for this book is available from
the British Library.

Printed and bound in Great Britain by Mackays of Chatham plc, Kent

Contents

Before the Days of Noah

Before the days of Noah
before he built his ark
seagulls sang like nightingales
and lions sang like larks.
The tortoise had a mighty roar
the cockerel had a moo
kitten always eeyored
and elephants just mewed.
    It was the way the world was
    . . . when owls had a bark
    and dogs did awful crowings
    while running round the park.
Horses baa-ed like baa lambs
ducks could all miaow
and animals had voices
quite different from now!
But came the day of flooding
and all the world was dark
the animals got weary
of living in the ark –
    So they swapped around their voices
    a trumpet for a mew
      – a silly sort of pastime
      when nothing much to do.
But when the flood had ended
and the world was nice and dry
the creatures had forgotten
how once they hissed or cried.

So they kept their brand-new voices
   – forgot the days before
   – when lions liked to giggle
and gerbils used to roar.

Missing Important Things

I didn't go to school this week
I stayed at home with Dad.
I didn't do a worksheet
and I am really rather glad.
I didn't do the number work,
I didn't do my words,
I didn't learn my spellings
and I didn't read my page.
I didn't go to school today –
we fixed the shed instead,
tied some flies and feathers
and dug the onion bed.
I saw the cat have kittens,
I climbed right up a tree,
mixed some sand and water
and held a bumblebee.
I didn't go to school all week
and I'm really not too sad –
I missed important lessons
and stayed at home with Dad.

Buzz Aldrin

Buzz Aldrin
when upon the moon
ate a dehydrated prune
then –
spat the stone upon the ground
as no one seemed
       to be around.

Since that day
the seed has grown
all around the moon-man's home.

And if you look on lunar nights
you'll see the moon man,
pale and white,
eating prunes
beneath the tree
where Mr Aldrin used to be.

Dear Teacher

Weather poems bore me,
trees that bend and sway,
frosted paths and grass
skies of blue and grey –
Clouds that scud or gather,
winds that rush and roar,
rain that beats and rattles,
blasts that slam the door.
I'm tired of misty mornings
and footprints in the snow,
ships and storms and rescues,
summer suns that glow.
I know about rainbows
and breezes by the score,
teachers might quite like them
but I've heard it all before.

You Are

The Oxo in the gravy,
the Bisto in my stew,
the custard on my pudding,
the window with a view.

You're the pressie in the cracker,
you're the apple in the pie,
the answer to the question,
the twinkle in the eye.

You're the magic in the secret,
my firework in the night,
my sunshine in the morning,
the sum that's always right.

You are neither rich nor famous
but to me you are the best –
you're the head upon my pillow
and the paw upon my chest.

World's End

Did you know the world is flat
and has a crumbly edge,
a bottom wrapped in brambles
and a honeysuckle hedge?
Its rims a rage of waterfalls,
buzzards, rabbits, rocks,
caverns, caves and hidey-holes,
the wombat and the fox.
It's a wonderland for playtime,
bungee jumps and kites
summer every morning
rainbows in the night.
It's a wilderness of wonder,
a place where no one goes
just nesting birds, and resting birds
the dodo and the rose.
    So – please don't tell the
                grown-ups.
They'll only spoil the place
with theme parks or a landfill
shops with world's-end lace.
Please – keep the edge our secret
the land that children found
and always tell your teachers
that their world is really ROUND.

Fairy Picnic

Under our kitchen table
on the new carpet
the fairies have prepared a picnic –
Tiny little cookies,
funny little cakes,
weeny little biscuits,
scrummy fairy flakes,
sarnies small as bee eyes,
pretty little buns.
It's called a fairy picnic . . .
But Mum says it's just crumbs.

Playground Duty

Adam and Eve
 at school
 one day
scurried out to morning play.
They ran and chased
for hours and hours
through summer suns
and winter showers.
They played for months
in wind and drizzle
as no one came
to blow the whistle.

A Viking Adventure
school from

A Walking-home-from-school Poem

Of course I don't like Darren,
I think he's really mad,
I think he's really stupid,
I think he's really sad.
OK, his smile's terrific
OK, his guitar's cool,
but I think Darren's useless
. . . I don't fancy him at all.
I really cannot stand him –
Darren's not my style.
But
I think that's him behind us,
so just slow down a while.

King Jude

King Jude was king
of the Lego
The pink and the blue
    and the white
The red and the green
    and the yellow
A ruler of wisdom and might
he built mighty towers
    and pavilions
His kingdom was cheerful and bright . . .
a servant called
Mummy attended
and swept up his cities
each night.

Big Billy

There's a spider in the bathroom
With legs as thick as rope.
It lives behind the cupboard
Where my mother keeps the soap.
My sister calls it Billy,
She says he creeps each night
Into children's bedrooms
(when they turn out the light).

I lay and hear him coming.
I hear his spider breath,
Huffing up the passage
With gasps as dark as death.
I hide beneath my duvet
. . . but the sides they won't tuck in . . .
And I know he'll find a pathway
And I know that Billy'll win!

I know he's going to get me.
I know he's going to come
And he's going to eat my sister
And he's going to get my mum . . .
He's going to eat the family,
He's going to eat us all
Cos Billy's really awful . . .

. . . and he's coming up the hall!!!

Excuses

It wasn't me who shot Cock Robin,
pushed Humpty Dumpty off the wall
or knocked Doctor Foster
(on his way to Gloucester)
into a puddle –
    IT WASN'T ME, MUM!
    IT REALLY WASN'T ME!
It wasn't me who laughed at the
buckles on Bobby Shaftoe's knee,
took the master's fiddling stick
or put little Tommy Tucker into the corner
with white bread and butter –
    IT WASN'T ME, MISS!
    IT REALLY WASN'T ME!
It wasn't me who put three men in a tub
and 24 blackbirds in the King's pie,
knocked Tommy Tucker's top knot off
or made all the town dogs bark –
    THAT WAS THE BEGGARS, SIR!
    THAT WAS THE BEGGARS . . .
    And please, sir,
it wasn't me who kissed the girls
and made them cry
or dropped the kitten down the well.
That was Georgie Porgie and Johnny Flynn . . .

And it was William Shakespeare,
Andrew Motion
and Roger McGough
doing kissin' –
they were there too, sir.
But I wasn't –
I was in the hills with Mary
looking for her lamb – sir.

The Collector

Not for me woolly dolls
or football cards
pop-star posters
model cars –
No, I'm into collecting adjectives.
     Big, fat, juicy, yummy, scrummy,
     rich and famous
     lean and keen
     kinds of words.
I store them up for special occasions
   in – massive, marvellous
      mysterious, magnificent
      adjectival boxes
  with secret seals
  and silver keys.
But, at the first stroke of the new millennium
my brother's bedside collection of marks
exploded with excitement
taking with them
the roof of our house
and
my adjective collection.

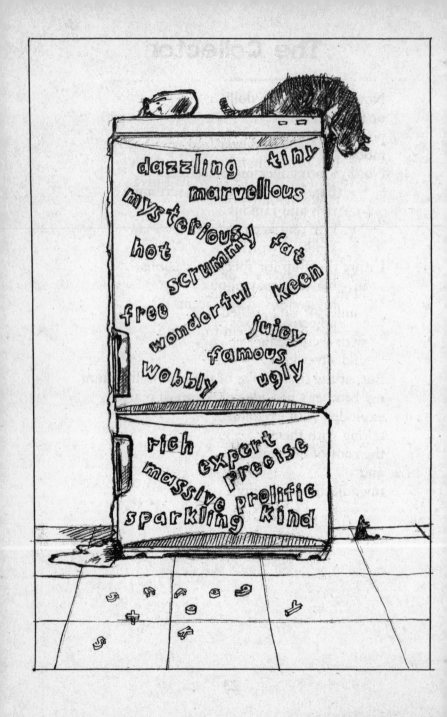

Request

If you should ever find an adjective
    it is probably mine.
You know the sort of word I mean
    lonely (cloud)
    misty (lace)
    sprightly (dance)
    pretty (place).
So if you ever see one
I'm sure it will be mine
unless it isn't spelled right
    – or doesn't seem to rhyme.

Famous Poets

Shakespearian poets
   wrote with quills
   to make some cash
   to pay their bills.

They wrote blank verse
   on parchment paper
   because computers
   came
   much later.

Guido Fawkes

Guido Fawkes
    (a funny name)
thought he'd like to gain
    some fame
and with some mates
    (a secret ring)
decided to explode the King.

The trick went wrong
as someone 'pooted'*
and poor old Guy
    was executed.

*A word they used in olden days
meaning 'to tell on someone'.*

Mr Roberts

Mr Roberts
      (morning prayers)
fell asleep
      (on teachers' chairs)
We all marched out
and went to classes
leaving him with snores
and glasses.
Come PE –
      (in the hall)
Mr Roberts missed it all
then quickly stood
      (at half past ten)
and shouted out
      a loud
          AMEN.

Yoostoobees

Come and see the 'Yoostoobees'
(they are things that 'used to be'):
   tigers
   whales
   and songbirds
when things lived wild and free.

They've got some plastic dolphins
that really swim and dive,
jars of ancient honey
from things they had called hives.

There's skeletons of hippos,
a fossil of a bear
that used to live in Greenland
in days when ice was there . . .

There's holograms of hedgehogs,
stuffed turtles and a snake,
a model of a meadow,
a swamp, a pond and lake.

It's a pity they've all gone now
but they all got in the way
of something called 'big business'
   and 'progress'
      so they say.

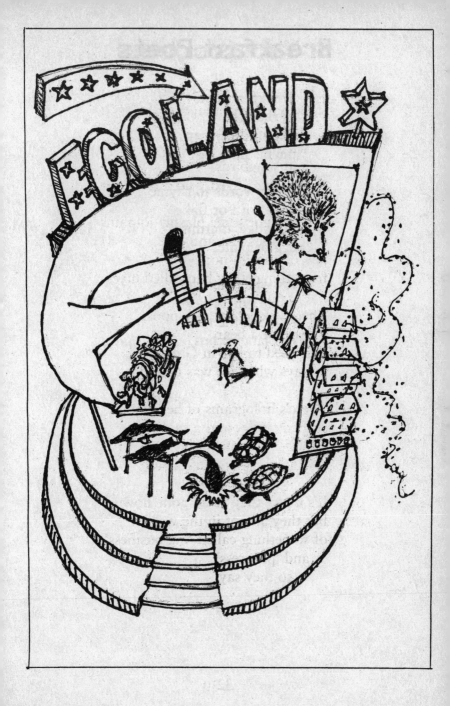

Breakfast Poets

Breakfast poets
as they chew
like to dream up
poems new.

Fresh words to rhyme
with corn or flake
porridge, marmite
egg or plate.

It's what they do
while others rush
to catch the train
or plane or bus.

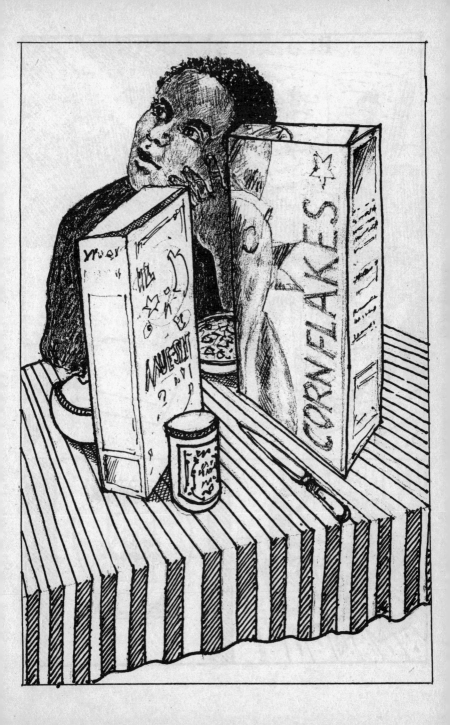

Diaries

Schoolboy's diary,   one small name,
                                        ink and crumple,
                                     smudge and stain.

Schoolgirl's diary,   fringed with lace,
                                        silver pencil,
                                     secret place.

Young man's diary,   brief and bold,
                                     student garret,
                                     crease and fold.

Girlfriend's diary,   evening light,
                                     words and wishes,
                                     sweet delight.

Soldier's diary,   battle cry,
                                     rank and number,
                                     'if I die . . .'

Lover's diary,   pink and blue,
                                     hearts and xxx

I love you

Manger

The servant girl brought water,
a lantern and some bread,
sweet hay for the infant,
a pillow for his head.
The pot boy welcomed strangers,
served them winter ale,
The inn man carved an angel
and hung it on a nail.

Holiday Swims

On Saltwick Nab
with teeth a-chatter
my father said
    'it didn't matter'
that northern seas
and icy breeze
should stab our flesh
and gnaw our knees.
    'Cold does you good'
he would explain
in a lash of wind
and a flail of rain.
    'It's really nice –
    come on in . . .'
balding head,
icy grin.

In dripping costumes made by mum
we'd struggle home from father's fun
and by warm fires
forget the pain
and plead that we might go again.

Stone-age School

In stone-age days
in stone-age schools
        (stone-age teachers
        stone-age rules)
it must have been a stone-large larf
        in maths or science
        or art and craft
to see the teachers standing there
in only bits of skin and hair!

And just imagine what a sight
the school would be on parents' night
        as mums and dads
        in pelts of creatures
stood in queues to see the teachers
        mammoth pants
        shirts that tickle
        itchy vests and socks that bristle.

My mum, your mum, dads galore
posey parents by the score . . .
        stone-age days
stone-age tables
stone-age clothes
        stone-age labels.

Icarus

With wax and feathers
just for fun
he tried to fly up to the sun.
'The wax is melting!'
(came a shout
as all his feathers fluttered out).

He fell to the ground
the end of Icarus . . .
inventive
brave
but quite ridiculous.

I Am

I am the finger pinched in the door
I am the wobble on the new bike
I am the shiver in the cold bath
the scare in the darkness
the slip on the stair.

I am the tangle caught in a comb
the lump in the custard
the stone in the shoe.

I am the lonely
the friend we forget
the kiss never given
the things we regret.

Mystery Poet

I love writing poems,
I've written a pile.
Some make you weepy
and some make you smile.
Some are for lovers,
soldiers or kings,
ladies with tresses,
pirates with rings.
   I've written of autumn,
   winter and spring,
   summer with roses
   and birds on the wing.
   I've written of sailors,
   faraway lands,
   angels in heaven
   with porcelain hands.
I've written of dragons,
castles and keys,
the wind in the willows,
peacocks and bees.
My first name is easy –
they just call me John
   but please call me Johnny –
   I'm Johnny.

Anon.

*A local school asphalted its
children's nature reserve.*

Collecting Time

They're filling in the toad hole
where we collected newts
They're filling in our toad hole
nets and jars and boots.
They're putting toads in buckets
they're going to set them free
in places that are useless
and toads don't want to be.
They're filling in our toad hole
and soon there's going to be
    a bigger
    better
    car park
for mum
her car
and me.

Excuses for Being
Late to School

The sun came out	– Snowman
I fell off a wall	– Humpty Dumpty
It was raining	– Noah's son
I saw a big spider	– Miss Muffet (reception class)
I met a wolf	– Little Red Riding Hood
I was looking for stones	– David the Shepherd
I went rowing with Daddy	– Grace Darling
Dad didn't wake me	– Rip Van Winkle's son
My dad took me to Nottingham	– Robin Hood's son
I went flying	– Peter Pan
I met a girl	– Hiawatha
I couldn't find my way	– Simple Simon
The sun was too hot	– Icarus
I was kissing some girls	– Georgie Porgie
I was writing this poem	– Peter Dixon

William

William was clever –
    he wrote things with a quill,
    tragedies and funnies,
    plays to scare and thrill.
He wrote of kings
    and lovers
    kisses
    battles
    wars . . .
Merchants, ghosts and witches,
the big, the weak, the poor.
William was clever
but Willie couldn't spell
and if he sat our SATs tests
then Will would not do well.

House Party

When the houses had a party
they invited all their friends –
the semis and the terraced,
the middles and the ends.
> They invited all the chalets,
> high-rise blocks of flats,
> caravans and castles,
> homes for dogs and cats.

They invited all the bungalows,
houses from Peru,
scrapers from Big Apple,
huts from Timbuktu.
> The igloos came,
> the tepees,
> the pagodas and a cave,
> an anthill
> and a beehive,
> a police house
> and a nave.

It was a lovely party –
the church house did some chants,
the summer house brought sunshine
and the greenhouse brought the plants.
> The lighthouse winked a message

PEACE

within each house
Hallelujah sang cathedrals
HALLELUJAH
> sighed the mouse.

50

Houdini

Houdini had a bad to-do
and locked himself
in Grandma's loo . . .
'Help!
I'm stuck!'
Houdini cried,
trapped securely tight inside.
'Twist the catch!'
my grandma said.
'Push the knob
that's painted red
kick the hinge
pull the slide
and then the door will open wide.'
Houdini wept,
Houdini sighed
but still Houdini stuck inside . . .
All day he stayed
all night as well
a week or more
I heard them tell
until he wriggled down the pan
up a drain
and said to Gran
'I'm out!
I'm here!
Houdini's free!
And I only went to have a pee.'

World-Book-Day Party

Welcome to the party
it's word day
     book day
     day . . .
There's going to be a party,
just step along this way.
Come and meet the party folk,
the Stories and the Rhymes,
the Couplets and the Novels,
the Chapters and the Lines.
The Epitaphs are coming,
Limericks of cheer,
the Adjectives and the Adverbs
(the Haikus too, I fear)!
So please try
     to get here early
     before the Annuals come,
     the Memoirs
     can be weary
     but the Anecdotes are fun.
You'll love just every moment,
the Brochures
and the Yarns,
the Journals,
and the Pamphlets,
the Sonnets
and the Psalms.
We're going to dance the Kenning,
play Flip-the-Tanka too!
Chuck around some Jingles
and catch the Clerihew.

It's going to be amazing,
we'll have a wicked time.
The word day,
     big day party
where we'll all
     rock and rhyme.

Whatever Happened To?

Whatever happened to inkwells
    inkpots
    blotters
    and spots?
Whatever happened to quill pens
    dip pens
    fountains
    with blots?
Whatever happened to smudges –
    on noses
    and fingers
    and toes
trickles of ink in the margins
kisses of ink on our clothes?
      I quite like a ball pen or biro
      A computer does everything fine
      but I'd rather be back with a quill pen
      and write in Shakespearean rhyme.

The Good Shepherd

Winter hillside
bite of cold
sheep and shepherd
warm in fold.
   Cosy shepherd
   rain and sleet
   sleeping shepherd
   nice warm feet.
Snoozy shepherd
starry sky
snoozy shepherd
hears a cry.
   One small cry
   one small bleat
   rock or thicket
   broken feet.
One good shepherd
crook and cape
rope and lantern
snick of gate.
   Lantern, shepherd
   rope on arm
   lamb and mother
   free from harm.
Folds warm welcome
mug of tea
shepherd's love
for you and me.

Olden-day Christmas Presents

Grandad says – when he was a boy
       all he had for Christmas
       was an orange
       and a pencil.

Grandma says – when she was a girl
       all she had in her stocking
       was a bag of nuts
       and a piece of coal.

Grandad's orange was for eating
and the pencil was for writing
his *thank-you* letter.
Grandma's nuts were for cracking
and the lump of coal was for luck.

It couldn't have been a very big piece.

Our Cat

After school today
    we buried Jasper
    with amber eyes
    and lazy ways.
Oliver
Olivia
Martha
Juliet and Alfie
were in attendance
also Grandma
who came late
because she could not find
her new camera.
    In his grave we placed
    a plastic bottle
    containing four new items
    one coin – new and dated
    a Grandma wooden clothes peg
    a small plastic soldier
    and a Dennis the Menace small badge.
Also our names
Oliver, Olivia, Martha, Juliet
and Alfie.
We had a silence.
And some sweets.
Why did he die? asked Alfie.
Where is heaven? said Olivia.
What is God? said Martha.
I understand all that – said Olivia
. . . but not the bottle bit.

Cana Party

It was a wedding party
with tons of food and wine
everybody dancing
a sunny lovely time . . .
until there was a murmur
until there came a shout . . .
'Something awful's happened –
the wine has just run out!'
A man who had been dancing
ordered, 'Pass that pot!'
(It was brimming full of water
but he didn't care a jot.)
He sort of poured and held it,
he sort of bowed his head
and the water turned to vino
a rich and vintage red.
The dancer smiled and nodded,
and quietly strolled away.
A teacher from the country,
I heard the bridegroom say.

Kings

William and Harold
   Henry, one to eight,
were famous Kings of England
at different times and dates.
They lived in pads called castles,
they slept in feather beds.
Some kings had a bad time,
others lost their heads.
   Richard went crusading,
   some just stayed at home,
   some were kind and friendly
   and others moaned and groaned.
   King George they called a farmer,
   Alfred burned the cakes,
   William was orange
   and Cromwell was a fake.
They loved to hunt and plunder,
they seemed to quite like wars,
flags and feasts and jousting,
parliaments and laws.
   But for me
   the best king ever,
   the one that I would choose,
   was the one with hips that swivelled
   who wore
      those blue suede shoes.

Magic Superstore

I know where all the magic's kept –
it's in a superstore,
it's called the magic market
and it's on the second floor.
    It's where witches do their shopping,
    wizards buy their brews,
    ogres get their mixes
    and boggarts stand in queues.
They put their buys in baskets,
push trolleys made of sticks,
full of horrid potions
and piles of dreadful tricks . . .
    The store's not very far from you,
    it's only down the lane,
    sharp left at the coven
    – left then right again.
Go past the cave of cobwebs,
be careful as you walk,
watch out for the vampire,
then take the second fork.
    You'll see the magic market,
    you'll smell it miles away
    and see the awful ogres
    who go there every day.
So:
go and buy some potions
and we'll mix some special brews
to turn us into princes
– and teachers into shrews.

PS Don't tell the others!

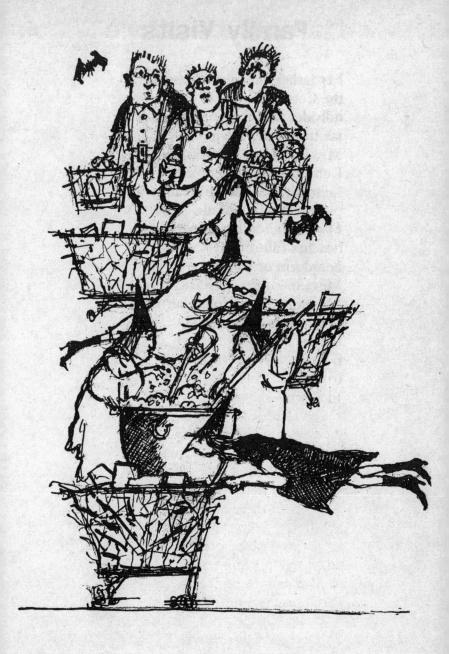

Family Visits

My father likes the country:
the Cotswolds, Dales and Downs,
hillsides where the sheep graze
far from busy towns.
My sister loves the seaside:
Runswick Bay or Poole,
sailing boats and ice creams,
piers and rocky pools.
My brother likes the sunshine:
beaches full of play
Benidorm or Corfu
Mexico – olé!
My mother does long journeys,
she asks us all to go . . .
but we refuse
politely,
to visit
El Tesco.

Wildlife

Cats are careful creatures,
they rarely slip or fall,
they hardly ever stumble
when padding down the hall.
It's just the same with goldfish,
they rarely tumble down
or slip upon a flagstone
when shopping in the town.
Creatures are so careful,
they seem to get things right,
no parachutes for pigeons
or lights for owls at night,
no maps for snails or swallows,
they never lose their way
travelling to Lettuce
or Val de l'Espirêt.
Wildlife's wise and wonderful
it could teach us many things
if we didn't chase
       or kill it
       . . . and shared the songs it sings.

Big Hunter

I'm really into hunting
I do it every day . . .
    I hunt the silky purple
    the woolly and the grey.
I hunt alone most mornings
underneath the beds,
    stalking after spotteds,
    the yellow and the red.
I hunt in scarlet dressing gown,
I call out 'tally-ho',
    sometimes in the bathroom
    or anywhere they go.
They're cunning and elusive,
they hide in secret holes,
    deep inside the duvet
    or in the blanket folds.
I rarely find them quickly –
they creep where no one dares
    and unless you're really lucky . . .
    they never hide

    in pairs.

Car-park Party

There's a party in the car-park
and it's going to be a hoot,
so polish up your bumper,
your whistle and your flute.

It's going to be tremendous –
the Ferraris will be there,
truckers with their trailers,
pickups from the fair.

There'll be go-karts by the bus load,
coaches full of fun,
taxis doing U-turns,
transporters by the ton.

It's going to be real crazy,
there's gong to be a slam –
caravans and hatchbacks,
motorbikes and vans.

The Rolls and Royce are coming . . .
so get yourself in 'pole' –
it's time to buy a ticket,
it's time to rev and roll!

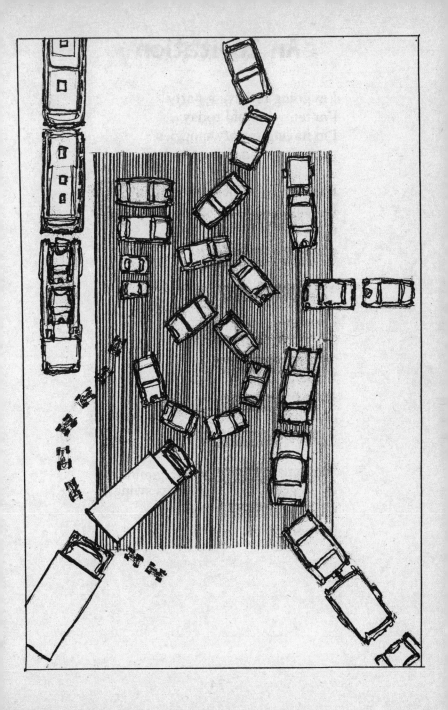

An Invitation

I'm going to have a party
I'm ten years old today
I'm having twenty moggies
to come and dance and play.

I've cooked some cod-head patties
I've made some frog-mince pies
some spider-leg spaghetti
and a pizza made with flies.

We're going to play cat's cradle
and curtain-climbing games
jumping up on tables
and making nasty stains.

We're going to sing some cat songs
– the bad cats will be there
and there's bound to be some fighting
with fur balls in the air!

It's going to be fantastic
we're going to make things swing
so slip into your catsuit
and come and do your thing.

Teddies

My teddies love to cuddle
my ellies, rabbits too,
my cats and frogs and turtles
my dragons and gnus.
They cuddle up so nicely
(they even hug the bee)
. . . but the really tricky problem
is that there's not much room for me!

ME!

The Human Knot

A man I know called Mr Muddle
tried to give himself a cuddle
   but arms and legs
   and bits that dangle
   wound into an awful
   tangle.

'I need some help!'
he gave a shout
and friendly folk came
running out.
They pulled, they pushed
but all in vain
his arms and legs just stayed
the same!
'Oh dear . . . !' he cried.
'What can I do?
I feel like something in a zoo!'

'Join us!' called Zippo.
'Be a star –
In our circus you'll go far!'
So now my friend's a different man –
and lives inside a painted van
A circus star
who earns a lot
and calls himself

THE HUMAN KNOT.

Waiting for Mum

Ink in my earhole
clay up my nose
dirt on my fingers
mud on my clothes . . .

Bright green painting
bright green hair
brand-new jacket
brand-new tear . . .

Waiting for my mother
we're going out to tea
I've a very funny feeling
she won't be pleased with me!

First Assembly

Teacher says that this morning
we are going to our first
assembly.
I don't want to go to assembly.
I didn't like the Tower of London much.
I won't like assembly.
I have got my money.
I have not got my packed lunch
or my swimming things . . .
and I don't want to go to assembly.
I want to stay here in my new school.
I like my new school
I like my new teacher
I like my new friends
and the hamster.
   I want to stay here.
   Anyway –
      I can't go to assembly
      because
      Mum's collecting me after school
      and we are going straight to
      Asda.

Last Assembly

At our last assembly
some children cried
and others blew their noses
pretended not to cry.
At our last assembly
Mrs Bailey got some flowers and a clap
because she was leaving
– to have a baby . . .
and Mr Morgan got a clap
because he was leaving
but not having a baby.
At our last assembly
Mrs Wiseman said it was
a sad day
and a happy day
and didn't get anything.
Mr Morgan got teacher-of-the-year award
but not a clap
because no one liked him.
At our last assembly we
stood for the last time
to sing the school hymn
but someone had put a football sock
in the piano
so we didn't.
At my last assembly
I got
my last detention.

School Sports Day

I'm not in the hurdles
I'm not in the sprints
I'm not in the skipping
   the throws
   or anything.
I'm not in the relay
sports day's what I dread
   but I know I'm for
   the high jump . . .
. . . for something that I said!

A TWIST IN THE TALE

Poems chosen by **Valerie Bloom**

A dazzlingly diverse collection of poems,
all with a twist at the end guaranteed
to surprise you!

Featuring gems from
Eric Finney,
Ogden Nash,
Kaye Umansky,
Vernon Scannell,
Jan Dean
and Paul Cookson
to name but a few.

A cynical man from Mauritius
Thought it foolish to be superstitious
When a black cat passed near
He stood firm, without fear
(What a shame that the panther was vicious).

Rachel Rooney

TAKING OUT THE TIGERS

Poems by **Brian Moses**

In this fantastic collection of poems,
Brian Moses tells us – in his inimitable style –
about tigers, teachers, witches, angels, conkers,
football, aliens, dinosaurs and hang-gliding
over active volcanoes!

from **Taking Out the Tigers**

At twilight time
or early morning
a tiger-sized ROAR
is a fearsome warning
as a huge cat swaggers
through a fine sea mist,
its paws the size
of a boxer's fist,
when they're
taking out the tigers
on Sandown beach.

THE COLOUR OF MY DREAMS
and other poems

by **Peter Dixon**

A stunning collection filled with gems that
will make you look at life from a
different angle.

from **The Colour of My Dreams**

I play my world of make-believe
I play it every day
and teachers stand and watch me
but don't know what to say.

They give me diagnostic tests,
they try out reading schemes,
but none of them will ever know
the colour of my dreams.

A selected list of titles available from Macmillan Children's Books

The prices shown below are correct at the time of going to press. However, Macmillan Publishers reserves the right to show new retail prices on covers which may differ from those previously advertised.

A Twist in the Tale		
Poems chosen by Valerie Bloom	0 330 39899 7	£3.99
Taking Out the Tigers		
Poems by Brian Moses	0 330 41797 5	£3.99
The Colour of My Dreams		
Poems by Peter Dixon	0 330 48020 0	£4.99

All Pan Macmillan titles can be ordered from our website, www.panmacmillan.com, or from your local bookshop and are also available by post from:

**Bookpost,
PO Box 29, Douglas, Isle of Man IM99 1BQ**

Credit cards accepted. For details:
Telephone: 01624 677237
Fax: 01624 670923
Email: bookshop@enterprise.net
www.bookpost.co.uk

Free postage and packing in the United Kingdom